Whispers of My Heart

Knowing God Series

KRISTIAN NELSON
WITH CHRISTINE NELSON

Whispers of My Heart

ISBN (e-book): 978-1-910986-19-6

ISBN (paperback): 978-1-910986-20-2

First published in 2019

by CN Publishing House

Kemp House,

152-160 City Road

London

EC1V 2NX

"And it came to pass that Kristian inquired of the Lord, and the Lord answered."

Contents

Foreword

It has been an absolute privilege, as a mother, to walk and continue to walk this journey with this honest, inquisitive and vivacious little man. I love the simplicity of Kristian's questions and I love the way our Father does not trivialize any of His questions but answers them bringing so much depth to Kristian and I believe to those who will read this book. It really unfolds to readers that we serve a God Who knows us intimately and wants to unveil Himself to us so we can truly have the right perception of Who He is and as a result know who we are and see others through His eyes. I would encourage every person to get a hold of this book and read it because it reveals to us adults what it means to be

childlike, unveils a unique perspective on how to get to know

God while revealing to us the heart of God page after page.

Whispers of My Heart unveils the natural ways that

God speaks to our hearts whilst disclosing His heart and His

Thoughts towards us. Inevitably, our belief of His truth

causes us to manifest an extended expression of who He is.

Thank you, Kristian, for the honour.

By Dr Christine Nelson

Introduction

I have been very sceptical about this God thing. I found it very difficult to believe many things because I could not see God. One day my Mum asked me, "if a new boy or girl started attending your school how would you get to know them?"

I answered immediately, "By asking questions."

Simple questions have helped me to know basic information and even interesting details. I started this journey when my Mum encouraged me to make it a habit of asking Jesus a question before I went to bed. The next day, she would ask me what I asked and what God had said in return. After I asked the question, I would wait in silence until He answered. This was, and still is, a great way for me to train myself to hear the voice of God and experience Him as He whispers to my heart. The scriptures have come alive to me and have helped to build my faith.

This book is part of my continued journey to know God. It has helped me, and I believe it will help you to know the voice of God for yourself. It includes journal sections for you to write your own notes from your own encounters as you begin or continue your journey of inquiring of the Lord.

Happy reading and journaling!

First Question

I asked that night, but I did not hear anything. The next day

I was speaking to my Mum about my question and she asked

me, "if God is the First and the Last how old is He?"

By my Mum's question I realised God was answering me.

You see, God was speaking through my Mum to answer me.

Scripture: Revelation 22:13b

"I'm A to Z, the First and the Final, Beginning and Conclusion."

(THE MESSAGE)

My jaw dropped when my Mum asked me the question.... I was so amazed at the thought that I was having because I realised God has no age! He was here before all of creation. He is the Final so He will be here even after. He is infinity....

I learnt a new word that day, "INFINITY". The dictionary tells us that infinity is described as being without bounds; limitless.

* * *

Why don't you ask God His age...?

Can you find scriptures that confirm what you heard?

How did you feel when you heard God's voice?

* * *

____

____

____

____

____

____

____

____

First Question

Second Question

Kristian: Where do you live?

God: Heaven

Heaven is what I heard. I was not sure if this was my own mind or God's, so I asked some more questions.

Kristian: Where is Heaven?

God: Heaven is in your heart.

Kristian: So, you live in my heart? That means you are tiny then...

God: Yes, I live in your heart. I am in you and you are in Me. I am not limited by size. I can be any size I want to be.

Kristian: WOWWWW!! (Still processing yet not sure I understood it all).

Scripture: John 14:20

"I will not leave you orphaned. I'm coming back. In just a little while the world will no longer see me, but you're going to see me because I am alive and you're about to come alive. At that moment you will know absolutely that I'm in my Father, and you're in me, and I'm in you.

(THE MESSAGE)

Kristian: (My mind going at 100 miles per hour) They will see You in me? I am never without you? How am I going to see you?

God: When you look with the eyes of your heart.

Kristian: The eyes of my heart?

God: Where is your heart?

Kristian: Within me (pointing to my chest).

God: Look from within

Kristian: Wow! (Still amazed yet puzzled).

God: When you look from within, you see what I see.

Kristian: Really?!

God: When you dream, that is you looking from within (inside out).

Kristian: So, can I see from within when I am awake?

God: Yes, be still and you will know.

Kristian: I don't know how to see from within....

God: To see from within is to meditate on truth - what is eternal. Whatever things are true, whatever things are noble, whatever things are just, whatever things are of good report.

I began to practice this... I began to ask Jesus what He sees when I am in my room, at church, at school, about a person and that really changed the way I was able to see. I choose to meditate on what He sees; I allow my heart to be taken over by it as I think it over again and again. Whatever He sees meditate on it. What you dwell on will determine what you see in your reality.

*   *   *

Practice seeing from within and begin to draw the images.

Describe what you see...

*   *   *

Second Question

Third Question

Kristian: I like to play computer games and watch videos.

God: You asked what I like to do... I take interest in every aspect of your life

Kristian: Everything?

God: Yes! I work all things out for your good.

Kristian: WOW! So even if it appears to be bad you can turn it around to work for my good.... (Still thinking).

God: Yes, I do. So even if it appears to be bad, know it is not beyond my reach. I never want you to live based on appearance (your five natural senses what you see, hear, feel, smell, taste) but on My Word, what I have said to you, what I have shown you, what I have magnified to you.

Scripture: Psalm 37:4

Delight yourself in the Lord,

And He will give you the desires

and petitions of your heart.

(THE MESSAGE)

Kristian: Because I am one with you, what You desire, I desire?

God: Yes, I am your Victory. To live from Me is to delight yourself in Me. I am your starting point.

* * *

What do you like to do?

How do you see God at work in what you like to do?

How are you living from God? Is He your starting point?

* * *

____

____

____

____

____

____

____

Third Question

Fourth Question

God: I made you in My image so I can do all you can do and

more. I am everywhere at the same time, all power is in Me,

everything that needs to be known I AM.

Kristian: WOW!

God: You see me every time you are true to who I say you are.

You are my image in visible form. When you submit to this

as truth you reflect all that I AM.

Kristian: I am Your image in visible form? So, when I am being disobedient who am I being?

God: That is a sign that you have forgotten who I say you are.

You only need to remember.

Kristian: Who do You say that I am?

God: All that I Am you are.

Kristian: WHAT!? Wow!

Scripture: 1 John 4: 17b

...as He is, so are you in this world.

(NKJV)

Scripture: John 17: 22

...The same glory [nature, character] **you gave me,**

I gave them,

So they'll be as unified and together as we are—

I in them and you in me...

(THE MESSAGE)

[Brackets added for emphasis]

Scripture: 1 John 2: 5

But the one who keeps God's word

is the person in whom we see God's mature love.

This is the only way to be sure we're in God.

(THE MESSAGE)

* * *

Who does God say that you are?

Meditate on the scriptures above... How have they helped you

to see your oneness with God?

Can you think of any other scriptures that reinforce this lack

of separation between you and God?

How do you live from this oneness in your daily life?

* * *

____

____

____

____

____

Fourth Question

Fourth Question

Fifth Question

Kristian: The Holy Spirit, The Father, Jesus, Yahweh, I AM, Jehovah Raphe.

God: Each of My names reveals a side of Me. The Holy Spirit reveals Me as a Spirit, Father reveals Me as your source of all things, Yahweh is My personal name which reveals Me as a God that is personable not one that is far away. I AM, reveals Me as the Ever-Present God that will always be with you.

Jehovah Raphe reveals Me as a God Who heals, restores, make all things new. I do not patch up when I restore it is always new. I am not a God that causes or takes delight in any form of sickness nor death or any form of oppression.

Kristian: You know people blame you for a lot of things?

God: Yes, it is because they have taken on a mistaken identity creating false images of Who I AM and as a result it veils their eyes from seeing me the way I Am.

Kristian: Are you saying that if we see ourselves wrongly it causes us to see You wrongly?

God: Yes, to see yourself wrongly shows you are not awakened to Me in that area of your life. So, that is why my many names unveil the truth of Who 1 Am in many ways.

Remember 1 said, you are My image in visible form. What you reflect in your behaviour is an indication of how you see Me. My children have carried false images of me in their hearts for centuries causing them to believe their mistaken identity as truth. When you truly know My names and what 1 represent, your behaviour changes because you begin to identify with the image you were made in. Kristian my boy, Love can only create love; Kindness can only create kindness and the list goes on. An image reflects after its own kind. Anything else is a lie.

Kristian: OH MY DAYZ!

* * *

What other names of God do you know?

What do they reveal to you about God's nature and

character?

Get into the habit of observing your behaviour...What does

your behaviour tell you about what you believe about God.?

* * *

____

____

____

____

____

____

Fifth Question

Sixth Question

Kristian: Hmm! What do you mean?

God: The devices that evolve are just a glimpse of the world I

live in, in My Kingdom. What these devices can do is what I

created you to do and what happens when those who walk in

their real identity not a mistaken identity.

Kristian: (Kristian shaking his head puzzled) What do you

mean?

God: Give me an example of a device you are thinking of?

Kristian: MacBook Air

God: What can a MacBook Air do?

Kristian: It has Facetime which allows me to speak to my Grandma face to face though she is miles away in the United States of America. Also, it has Siri that you can ask questions and he answers. You can talk into the MacBook Air and it will type for you.

God: Everything you have mentioned begun with ME. I introduced Facetime a long time ago. Can you remember when Adam and Eve were in the Garden? I spoke to them face to face. I have always valued face to face greatly, rather than hearsay.

Siri can help you with lots of things; however, I sent you the Holy Spirt Who is a built in Helper to you to remind you of what you think you don't know but have only forgotten. Siri can help you with some things, but the Holy Spirit will help you with all things.

You mentioned that the device can write for you but everything you see around you was once invisible, in my mind, but now they are made visible.

Kristian: Wow! You are greater than any device! Anything a device can do; you have been doing it forever and ever. You can do it better than any device could even try. WOW!

* * *

Can you think of any device you have and its features that

you want to ask God about?

Maybe for you it is not a gadget or a device but something

else that you are amazed at? What is it for you? Why not ask

God about it? Is it greater than God in you in your eyes?

Are you more amazed at this gadget or device more than

God?

* * *

____

____

____

____

Sixth Question

Seventh Question

Kristian: Yes but...what kind of food?

God: Every time Heaven and Earth synchronize or work as

one, I am satisfied just like when you eat and are filled. Every

time what I dreamt or envisioned is fulfilled or becomes your

reality; perfection or completion is manifested. What is and

what has always been will continue to unfold before the eyes

of those who are awakened that will continue to be a great

joy.

Scripture: John 4:32-39

He told them, "I have food to eat you know nothing about."

The disciples were puzzled.

"Who could have brought him food?"

Jesus said, "The food that keeps me going is that I do the

will of the One who sent me, finishing the work he started.

As you look around right now, wouldn't you say that in about

four months it will be time to harvest?

Well, I'm telling you to open your eyes and take a good look at

what's right in front of you. These Samaritan fields are ripe.

It's harvest time!

"The Harvester isn't waiting. He's taking his pay, gathering in this grain that's ripe for eternal life. Now the Sower is arm in arm with the Harvester, triumphant. That's the truth of the saying, 'This one sows, that one harvests.' I sent you to harvest a field you never worked. Without lifting a finger, you have walked in on a field worked long and hard by others."

Many of the Samaritans from that village committed themselves to him because of the woman's witness: "He knew all about the things I did. He knows me inside and out!"."

(THE MESSAGE)

Kristian: WOW! So, your food is spiritual? That day when the Samaritan believed Jesus, that was food for Jesus?

God: Yes, my greatest joy is to see My offspring be who I say

that they are.

Kristian: Is that why you told Peter to feed your sheep?

God: Yes, teach them truth. Let them know how much I love

them. Let them know that they are my greatest thought, my

greatest treasure, always will be my greatest manifestation.

"Where your treasure is there your heart will be also."

* * *

What is your greatest treasure?

What brings you the greatest joy?

* * *

____

____